Our Burdened World

Vivian Kearney

ISBN-13: 978-1-63065-128-2

PUKIYARI PUBLISHERS
www.pukiyari.com

Thanks to:
Milo, my husband,
our daughter, Kathleen Anzak,
our son, Sean Kearney, Inkie Gillian,
Ninfa Kohler and others who have contributed
thoughts for this book,
to Ian Kearney, Collin Kearney and Stephen
Maldonado for their thoughtful poems,
and to Ani Palacios Mc Bride,
our patient and helpful editor.

Dedicated to Milo
(we've been married 50 + years this year), our
children, grandchildren, families,
and the caregivers and helpers and the people
who have suffered and died
during this year's worldwide contagion.

Table of Contents

Staycation

A trip into a stay in place
That everyone needs to take
All over the world

Waiting for the all-clear word
Each wondering what
Hidden silver linings
Will be missed

In the sometime to be
Old normal time

Lockdown Views

Our street has become a quiet village
Mostly everyone
Contained inside hushed houses

Except when
Neighborly friendliness
Timed but concerned
Reaches out

Except for many
Dogs on leashes, smiling
Incredibly happy for
The bonanzas of attention,
Exercise, sniffing adventures

Except for two young people
Strolling on the sidewalk
Profiting from the early evening's
Late sunlight

No students, however
Who attend
The nearby Junior High
In sight

Grocery Scene

Cravings, insatiable cravings
That everyone has
All at once
For targeted items
(today pizzas and croutons)

Presenting us with
Depressing metal
Of empty shelves

Was it some signal heard or seen
To buy identical, hitherto humble
Must-have specialties

Or, have we each received
The same list in the same dream?

Isolating Together

Our now closer world
Is threatened

By an invisible, murderous
Enemy with hooks ready
To tear our cells apart

We are trying to
Isolate together

Hoping for stronger,
Benevolent
Immune systems
To bail us out

The Skies of Yesteryear

We didn't realize
We were riding high horses
Of privilege

Flying in storied realms
Beyond mere provision, security
That others were and are desperate
To find

We used to shop laden stores that
Sold more goods than imagined
In some people's
Wildest dreams

Where did
The skies of yesteryear
Disappear?

And if our
Previous way of life
Could reappear

Should we
Adopt it again?

Keep Calm, Sail On

Adventuring
Differently
At this stage
Of willing quarantine

On another
Inner sea
With its own waves
And possibilities

Still the moon
And the sun
Witness God's
Amazing charity

Anti-Intuitive Tense Wishes

Hope for the past
Nostalgia for the future
That previous blessings can last
For a long, long time
That tomorrow's lessons
Help yesterdays endure

One Possibility

During this waiting game
Of uncertainty

Worrying what will happen
To our families, our species

One internet-advised
Project activity

Says: You can start with
Notes to self
To write, keep on writing

Concerns sadly,
Thanks gladly

With threaded words

To repair
Some of your once sheltering
Goals, routines

Now partially shredded
Tent of identity

Didn't Used to Be

Virtually,
Virtuously

I wander down the
Grocery aisles

Picking and choosing
Enjoying the colors
Packaging and textures

In my mind

To be bought by proxy
By our ever more dear family
During quarantine

Yet They Noticed

Even with faces
Half-hidden by masks
And six feet apart
Everyone tries to smile

Waiting patiently at check-out
Calmly perusing grocery aisles

For, it seems a treat
To visit food stores
Every once in a while

A revered outing
Not harried or humdrum
To be enjoyed

Then, back home,
Conversing, playing cards
With sons and their girl friends
Somewhat at loose ends

Yet that extra time together
A blessing to remember

And Counting

This long sheltering
Who knew it could last for more
Than three months lonely

For Our Part

At the start
For our part
As if preparing for a hurricane

We emptied store shelves
To calm ourselves
Successively stockpiling
Special items

As if they'd go extinct
Or disappear

Which they did
By self-fulfilled prophecies

Although the illness and
Lonely deaths
By parasite

That we try to avoid
Are tragically real
For numerous people
And their families

The House and Hibernation

The house where
We must hibernate

Tries to replace
Our family, friends
Acquaintances, neighbors
Since now we must
Stay six feet apart
If we go out

With its close corners conversing
Its well-known walls comforting
Its spacey projects calling

While the radio, newspaper,
TV and computer screen
Tell us stories

Announcing cases for optimism
But also pessimism
Sometimes both at once

However, how to tell our home
It still can't socialize
Barter, help or sympathize
As humans do

Different Instructions

– So, children,
How do you like
Our new lives at this time?

I tell you to take out your tablets,
Activate your cell phones
Go to your computers
Do your lessons on line

How do you like this
Different type of instruction?

 – Well, The first two weeks I was happy
To be staying at home
The next few weeks were fine
But now this change is getting old

I miss seeing my friends
Some teachers and classes
Were cool too

And even when they weren't
It was good to complain
Together

Yes!
I'm definitely ready
To share the ups and downs
Of learning journeys
Even worksheets and tests
At my school

Teachers From Home

Teachers, how about you
With your profession's demands new
With all your preparations due

For lessons, documentations
Course guidelines, materials
Even before the classes start?

– We were nervous at first
Now we've acquired
The desired ease

To show students individual care
To encourage them to share
Problems and roadblocks with

The quality of their internet
Possibilities for their localities
Questions about their lessons

In this modern technological
Educational world
Before, during and after

Such a momentous turn-around
With our much to be taught
Talked and learned about
Our 2020 world-wide challenge

We've Been So Deprived

We've missed you all
We've been so deprived

Cousins, friends, family
How good it is to see you, to talk
In the same space
For a while

Please don't only drive by

Hope we never take real meetings
And social times for granted again
When these months of confinement
Pass by

Scapegoat
(by Ian Kearney)

Solemnly staring at the sunset,
There was hope for a new day
Laughter and joy were almost in sight
But Death had something to say:

"Your foundation is weak, your beliefs muddled
The rock of your church has begun to crumble.
'Tis not your time, 'tis not your hour
This year will indeed be nothing but sour."

In the following months, death reaped with his scythe
The disease could be fatal but wasn't the only blight
As people despaired, fools searched for a scapegoat.

Politicians looked to the east
Claiming bats were the beast
That shattered and hammered the earth to its knees.

Still others searched inward in spite of their fear,
And looked for another to blame for this year.
They strained their baffled brains
Searching for something.

"But of course!" One dunce chimed in
"To distract, let's attack
Let's blame those with melanin
For… whatever"

Race was determined by the weak to be the enemy
The 19th century reared its head once more
While they hunted for a remedy.

The chaos was doubled
The violence ensued.

Now what have we left but our own views?
In these trying times, the only right thing
Is to put yourself in your neighbor's shoes.

No one is to blame,
Except everyone
And we must make peace
So that reconciliation
Can be done

A New Mo(u)rning
(by Collin Kearney)

The sun rises, I am awake
The whole rest of the day is mine to take

The birds are chirping, the sky is lit,
But there is no one to appreciate my humor and wit

My brother sleeps 'till one
My mother began work before the rise of the sun

My father is tired of my jokes
While some say this is all a hoax

I am alone
Most will cry and moan

But, I will persevere
When others are drenched with fear

As the deaths goes up and hope is lost
I ask: "What will be the final cost?"

While lives fall, there are prayers for all
For this may have started small

But we must last a little longer
So our antibodies can get stronger

Claustrophobic
(by Stephen Maldonado)

Stuck inside, he is glassy-eyed
Nowhere to go, no one will show
He feels alone

Time has slowed down to a crawl
Rendered inert by a chain and ball
What have we done to it all?

Left alone with his thoughts for far too long
Distractions don't last forever, so go ahead, listen to a song
Before neuroticism grips him like searing tongs

Since

Since, presently
We have realized
Our amazing similarities
With our global neighbors
No matter how far away

Everyone being
Constrained to wear masks
Wash hands often,
Respect distances

And we really wish
All would stay inside
Healthy and wise
Adopt smaller footprints
Not shop so much
Let the earth rest
From our depredations

Will we keep
This sympathy for others
Work to give this planet
A Green New Deal

And, with our novel compassion
Legislate Medicare, education,
Transportation, livable incomes,
Cities, places, consideration for all

Saints and Angels

Doctors, ministers, nurses, pharmacists,
Medical, safety, grocery, transportation workers
And the many amazing volunteers
Helping humanistic causes

Are some of today's saints and angels
Certainly deserving thanks and applause

Also health-oriented, wise legislators
(As are some)
In this fearful time

Actually, we can all activate
The compassionate side
Of our brains, character

Moved and lit
By God's holy, loving Spirit

Meditating Prompt

This restricting season
Reflecting on reflections
Of the windows picturing
Vistas of trees beyond

Their branches telling
A drama of summery leaves
Dancing with the breezes

All mirrored on half of
The blackened TV screen

A show put on by nature
Come into our living room
To entertain
Two-dimensionally

To meditate on
And while away some minutes
Of this open-timed
Quarantine

Mind-Expanding

Presently when
Meeting people rarely
Or riding out
Into the bright, quiet streets

Those occasions
Seem so implausibly
Other-worldly

Psychedelic and mind-expanding
Filled with vivid colors
And sparkling graces

Scarcely earned
By sheltering in place

For weeks and months
To heal our poor,
Warned, sickened
Fault-ridden world

Activists

We are one small fragile planet
Said the hippies of the sixties

Wrote Rachel Carson,
Explain scientists

Exclaim Greta and the youth
Of today
And people, politicians
Not under corporations' sway

Whose loud, profiteering greed
Pulled materialistic wool
Over our eyes and ears

Yet, somehow,
A minute, malevolent parasite
Got our attention
(Though for how long?)

And we see we all need
Kinder, wiser spirits
For the health of our
One small fragile planet
And everyone on it

What to Think?

Is this a sign of
Animals, nature
Getting their revenge?

Or is this contagion
A lesson from God?

Therefore, will angelic
Acts of goodness

Help to heal
Our burdened world?

Made Visible

The brittle, subliminal
Machinery that keeps
Societies going, calling for
Cooperative interdependence

Has been made visible
By infectious,
Quite visible agents

So many complex details
Supporting our civilizations
We should have known

Realized and reworked before
For the good of all

A Sheltered Place

A green, clean
Country area
With pristine air
Crystalline lakes
Lovely trees

The inhabitants, content and proud
Of their careful population
Sheltered space

Too beautiful, too beckoning
Not to appeal
To outsider city-dwellers
Searching for refuge
Far from illness-
Transmitting crowds
For their second homes

Soldiers tried to stop
This escapist onslaught
Or at least test
Those unwelcome newcomers
Requesting health certificates

Yet, finally
One case of infection
So feared
Did appear

An uninvited tourist
Contaminating
This impossibly Elysian
Shangri-La

For, the entire planet
With all its people
Is this dangerous malady's
Hunting ground

Who Knows?

Who knows who
Will survive
On the other side
Of this months-long pandemic

When will we know when
It's safe to go back
To our previous lives
In a normal world
Yet on better, kinder tracks

How will we know how
To cope with and eradicate
Those agents of doom

Who can tell us why
And whence this curse
Or when will it be lifted

From all lands, all people
By the Son of love
From above

Like Dali's Clocks

Much like Dali's clocks
Time has been hung out
To dry
In deserts
And inside

Our calendars of work
And celebrations
Exiled
For a while

Since the days
Melt into each other

Marked only
By the sun, moon, stars
Seasons
And growing grass

That tell us
– This planet needed a rest
From your destructive
Walls of denial

All your anthropocentric
Human-centered
Algorithms and
Measured dials

Contradictions

A week passes quickly, like a day
A day meanders slowly like a week

We are kept apart by social distancing
Yet feel more affinity
Than ever before
To neighbors around the world

With so much information
We have discovered
Through media and technology
How little we know

How few defenses we have
Despite our weaponized
For inequality
Economy

Turnarounds

On the other hand
This lazy, hazy life
Has its attractions
As we take multiple naps

In this added retreat
Nestled abruptly,
Within our retirement
That we were just
Getting used to

And we experience
Surprizing turnarounds
With our kids worried about
Their elderlys' absences

When we go AWOL from home
Forgetting to announce outings
For batteries, gas, medicine

Trips so exciting now
So forgettable before

Overarching Prayers

Events and reactions
May be global from now on
We may mourn failures
In far countries
Communicate our worries with
No longer strangers

Island retrenchment
Nativist proclamations
Fragmenting propensities
Superficial quandaries

Will make much less sense
Than prayers for world health
And peace

Less Consumerism

This confinement leaves me not coveting
Quite as many goods as before
Just a few items from a few stores
So that the usual balance can be restored

Though with more than usual thoughts and prayers
For all people, this planet, more appreciation
Wise stewardship from leaders and nations
With better values and healed foundations

Hamlet's Thrift versus
Madonna's *Material Girl* Song

Novel frugality
Or previous storing and collecting
Vindicated

Stretching drinks with water
Wondering how can re-use
Perfectly good empty containers
Find low-tech entertainment
Forego the latest fashions
Shop our surprising closets

Recycling versus consumerism

Will we, will I
Return to retail therapy
When some of the
Old normal comes back

And make ourselves, shops
And corporations happy
For a while

Maybe we're getting closer to
Hamlet's speech on thrift
And away from Madonna's clarion call

Other Changes

Even the Internet
Now recommends
That we read classic works
In the paper book
More personal format

And Zooming with
People on screen

Not quite as cool
As meeting with
So-missed others
Three dimensionally
In reality

Meanwhile, Our Feathered Friends

Have you heard
Chirped the birds
On the quiet streets

People are staying
Many are praying
Inside
Using less gas

We can come back
Isn't this a lark
We can hear ourselves sing

Despite humans' depredations
Endless urbanization

They aren't invincible
After all

Unforeseen

We might acquire
A special shyness gene

When shields
Are no longer required

And our faces' natural masks
Are once again
In full view

Another Scenario

Babies, moreover
So used to people with a mask
May ask yet without words

 – What's happening?
Or may cry

When we stop
Covering our faces

Wondering how and why
Adults would walk
Around in public

Like that

Once Upon a Time

Once upon a time
I used to visit
Some clothes shops

Previous retail therapy
You're still good to me

Unexpected and useful home finds
Help my staycation nerves unwind

And keep the calm
To pray that all
Be provisioned and blessed

Losing Unhealthy Set-Points – Philippians 4:8

When
My eating schedule
Works out well

And I lose weight
Get a lot done
Can help

I try to turn that lesson
Into a useful routine
Proprietary habit

But the old personal set-point
Returns to take its place
So persuasively, so quickly

………………..

Now that our world
With its markets, communities
Has been disrupted

Will we return as a society
To our habitual destructive set-points
Good only for the selfish and wealthy

Or even descend to worse
Policies, inequalities

Lord, help us climb higher
And whatever is good, healthier,
Just and true
Think and do

Calendar Ever Faster

Despite this contagion-caused pause
Stretching the hours

My nature-themed wall calendar
Seems to move ever faster, flipping
From one monthly photo to another

Of wonders all around
But I can't meditate
On each beautiful picture
For too many days

Since these timeless months
Don't want to slow down

WWJD (What Would Jesus Do?)

Cell destroyer, whom will you
Prove right or terribly wrong
Strong, careful health measures or
A hurried, worried economy?

Can legislators and individuals
Choose wisely and charitably?
In this sad, strange time …
What would Jesus do?

General Hopes

As this world struggles
With a minute, terrible
And well-armed parasite

Once-persuasive commercials
Seem now too bland and tone-deaf
To keep their consumer hooks sharp

While the changed
General hopes endure
That silver linings would stay

Such as cleaner air,
Friendlier interactions
Kinder policies
That fix economic inequalities
Healthier habits
Quickened scientific work
For medical cures

Even as we wait
For this planet-wide death cloud
To be vaccinated and blown away

MOPLA (Make Our Planet Livable Again)

There are

Stealthy cell mines
Microscopic explosives
Walk and clean carefully

Now we have this contagion's name
We know its nefarious game
To attack and proliferate

Lean on kind helpers
Learn from wise persons
Humbly and gratefully

Let's not be dismissive
Nor address the dangers
Too little or too late

Let's make this planet
With God's Holy Loving Spirit
Great and livable again

www.ingramcontent.com/pod-product-compliance
Lightning Source LLC
Chambersburg PA
CBHW021914040426
42447CB00007B/849